Changing the Atmosphere

By: Brad Burk

Acknowledgements

Cover Graphic: Jordan Burk
ISBN: 978-1530191604
© 2016 Brad Burk
Printed in the United States of America
Changing the Atmosphere
Published 2016 by Brad Burk, Dallas, Texas

Dedication

I want to honor my father, Bo Burk, who always encouraged me to follow after God by reading His Word and seeking His face. His greatest advice was that as I read the Bible, I needed to always consult the author as to what it really says. Following my father's advice and wisdom came the revelation of the ability to change the atmosphere by words of blessing.

I want to thank Chris and Bill Davis for inspiring me to write this book. Never giving up on me, but always encouraging me to share the revelation that has challenged many to rethink how words truly can change their world. Chris has been faithful to pray while Bill faithfully spent hours formatting the book after it was written. I am very grateful for their dedication in helping me prepare a key that will bring hope and insight into the kingdom of God that will be life-changing.

I also want to dedicate this book to the numerous people who have urged me to put into writing the revelations God has given me over the years. Time and time again I have heard, "This needs to be a book!" Now is the season I felt released to write. Thank you so much for all your support and encouragement.

I want to thank my heavenly Father for giving me the anointing of a ready-writer. To Him be all glory, honor and praise.

Enjoy the journey!

Foreword

Brad Burk is a prophet with an unusually powerful prophetic gifting. I usually hear him teach on something and then three years later other ministers will begin teaching the same thing. For two decades Brad and Melba Burk have been wonderful friends to my husband Bill and I. We intensely value their friendship because they are truly seekers of God. Everyone can now experience the joy of being touched by God through Brad and his first book, <u>Changing The Atmosphere.</u>

The message in this book is potent and will incite thought, heart, and action in the Body of Christ! This book is destined to become a classic and is very timely in a world where we desperately need to change the atmosphere over our lives, our families, our cities and our nation. This book of hope and revelation will transform you from the darkness of distress to destiny...it is a must-read. The enemy is really going to hate this book! That makes me love, <u>Changing the Atmosphere,</u> all the more!

Chris Davis
Author of <u>Blessings Bring Change</u>, <u>New Testament Giving</u>, <u>Women in the Ministry</u>, <u>Walking in Your Kingdom Identity</u>, <u>Fear of the Lord</u>, <u>Love</u>, <u>Chart Your Course By The Dream In Your Heart</u>, <u>Rest Refreshing and Fire</u>,

Yakima, WA

Table of Contents

BEWARE! BEWARE! THE BRIDGE IS OUT!

INTRODUCTION

I hope I didn't startle you too much, but I wanted to get your attention. If you are like me, I have always had the tendency to skip over the introduction and go straight to Chapter One. Over the years I realized that I was missing an important part of the book by not reading the introduction, which usually is the foundation of the text. Such is the case here. But I also wanted to bring up the fact that many of us are stuck or stagnant, and cannot seem to move forward. There seems to be a bridge out that keeps us from getting to the other side as we move toward our destiny. I believe this book can help you build or repair the bridges in your life.

There is a verse in the Bible that I have read for years, but I have to admit, I really didn't believe it. Although I didn't realize it, the truth was that if I really believed it I would have been practicing it. The verse is Proverbs 18:21.

Proverbs 18:21
Death and life are in the power of the tongue, and they who indulge in it shall eat the fruit of it [for death or life]

I have no problem in understanding what life and death are. But the balance of that power is in the tongue? I always heard that sticks and stones may break my bones, but words will never hurt me. Turns out it is an absolute lie! Contained in this book are some instructions as to how our words can work for us, and that words are also powerful enough to bring life or death.

Is it not interesting that the Bible is full of verses that not only warn us about the tongue, but also instruct us on how to use the tongue? With so many verses about our mouth, shouldn't we be a lot more serious about what comes out of it? I would urge all us to do an in depth study on all the Bible passages that pertain to the tongue. Consider prayerfully what it says in James 3.

James 3: 1-18

Not many [of you] should become teachers (self-constituted censors and reprovers of others), my brethren, for you know that we [teachers] will be judged by a higher standard *and* with greater severity [than other people; thus we assume the greater accountability and the more condemnation]. For we all often stumble *and* fall *and* offend in many things. And if anyone <u>does not offend in speech</u> <u>[never says the wrong things]</u>, he is a fully developed character *and* a perfect man, able to control his whole body *and* to curb his entire nature. If we set bits in the horses' mouths to make them obey us, we can turn their whole bodies about. Likewise, look at the ships: though they are so great and are driven by rough winds, they are steered by a very small rudder wherever the impulse of the helmsman determines. <u>Even so the tongue is a little member,</u> <u>and it can boast of great things</u>. See how much wood *or* how great a forest a tiny spark can set ablaze! <u>And the tongue is a fire</u>. [The tongue is a] <u>world of wickedness set among our members,</u>

13

contaminating and depraving the whole body and setting on fire the wheel of birth (the cycle of man's nature), being itself ignited by hell (Gehenna). For every kind of beast and bird, of reptile and sea animal, can be tamed and has been tamed by human genius (nature). But the human tongue can be tamed by no man. It is a restless (undisciplined, irreconcilable) evil, full of deadly poison. With it we bless the Lord and Father, and with it we curse men who were made in God's likeness! [10] Out of the same mouth come forth blessing and cursing. These things, my brethren, ought not to be so. Does a fountain send forth [simultaneously] from the same opening fresh water and bitter? Can a fig tree, my brethren, bear olives, or grapevine figs? Neither can a salt spring furnish fresh water. Who is there among you who is wise and intelligent? Then let him by his noble living show forth his [good] works with the [unobtrusive] humility [which is the proper attribute] of true wisdom. But if you have bitter jealousy (envy) and contention (rivalry, selfish ambition) in your hearts, do not pride yourselves on it and thus be in defiance of *and* false to the Truth. This [superficial] wisdom is not such as comes down from above, but is earthly, unspiritual

(animal), even devilish (demoniacal). For wherever there is jealousy (envy) and contention (rivalry and selfish ambition), there will also be confusion (unrest, disharmony, rebellion) and all sorts of evil *and* vile practices. But the wisdom from above is first of all pure (undefiled); then it is peace-loving, courteous (considerate, gentle). [It is willing to] yield to reason, full of compassion and good fruits; it is wholehearted *and* straightforward,
impartial *and* unfeigned (free from doubts, wavering, and insincerity). <u>And the harvest of righteousness (of conformity to God's will in thought and deed) is [the fruit of the seed] sown in peace by those who work for *and* make peace [in themselves and in others, that peace which means concord, agreement, and harmony between individuals, with undisturbedness, in a peaceful mind free from fears and agitating passions and moral conflicts].</u>

I could write another whole book about this passage alone, but I will refrain for the moment. What I do want us to glean from this chapter is that our destinies lie in the power of our tongues. Whether we are a ship or a horse, it does not matter. If our rudder or bridle (tongue or mouth) is not handled properly, we will end up on the rocks, or riding head first off a cliff. Please take the Bible seriously. It was written to give us good days. We may not be necessarily just talking about our salvation, but we are talking about enjoying the journey.

Brad Burk

Psalm 119:2
Blessed (happy, fortunate, to be envied) are they who
keep His testimonies, and who seek, inquire
for *and* of Him *and* crave Him with the whole heart.

Proverbs 10:6
Blessings are upon the head of the
[uncompromisingly] righteous (the upright, in right
standing with God) but the mouth of the wicked
conceals violence.

Proverbs 16:20
He who deals wisely *and* heeds [God's]
word *and* counsel shall find good, and whoever leans
on, trusts in, *and* is confident in the Lord—happy,
blessed, *and* fortunate is he.

1

What We Hear, Say, and Pray

Sometimes we overlook the simplest things as Christians because we view the Bible as being too deep and mysterious to understand. Actually, I believe the Bible was intended by God to communicate with the average person. Although there are mysteries held in the Word of God, we as Christians are able to receive and understand them as we prayerfully seek the presence of God. From the beginning of time God has always wanted to communicate directly with his people. Look what He said to Moses in Exodus 19.

Exodus 19:5-8
Now therefore, if you will obey <u>My voice</u> in truth and keep My covenant, then you shall be My own peculiar possession *and* treasure from among *and* above all peoples; for all the earth is Mine. And you shall be to Me a kingdom of priests, a holy nation [consecrated, set apart to the worship of God]. These are the words you shall speak to the Israelites. So Moses called for

19

the elders of the people and told them all these words which the Lord commanded him. And all the people answered together, and said, All that the Lord has spoken we will do. And Moses reported the words of the people to the Lord.

God wanted His people to be able to hear His voice and to have a close relationship with Him. The people responded and said "Yes" to God's proposal. It was at this time in Exodus 20, God gave Moses the Ten Commandments. The Ten Commandments were not necessarily laws that must be obeyed, but an overview of the relationship God wanted His people to have with Him and with others. The Ten Commandments are all about mankind's relationship, first with God, and then with his fellow human beings. But, when He did speak to them from the mountain, they changed their mind about hearing the voice of God first hand and wanted Moses to hear for them. It has been that way ever since. People want someone else to hear God for themselves and then decide if that person really hears God. This way they can blame any wrongdoing or disobedience on someone else's ability to hear. It's called not wanting

to take responsibility for our own relationship with
God.

Exodus 20:19
And they said to Moses, You speak to us and we will
listen, but let not God speak to us, lest we die.

You may be saying, "That was the Old Testament."
What about today? God has not changed His mind.
The very reason that Jesus came and died was to
restore us to the Father the way that He always
wanted us. He still wants a relationship with His
people and to be able to communicate with them.
But, can we really communicate with God today? The
Bible tells us because of what Christ did for us we *can*
hear His voice.

John10: 3-5
"The doorkeeper opens [the gate] for this man, and
the sheep hear his voice *and* pay attention to it.
And [knowing that they listen] he calls his own sheep
by name and leads them out [to pasture]. When he
has brought all his own *sheep* outside, he walks on
ahead of them, and the sheep follow him because
they know his voice *and* recognize his call. They will

never follow a stranger, but will run away from him, because they do not know the voice of strangers."

This clearly tells us that we as Christians can hear the voice of God, as long as we go through the door by way of the Doorkeeper, which is Jesus. Jesus wants to lead and guide us throughout our life, so we can fulfill our calling and destiny. Maybe you are wondering how this can happen? The book of Ephesians gives a wonderful insight into how this works.

Ephesians 1:11
In Him we also were made [God's] heritage (portion) *and* we obtained an inheritance; for we had been foreordained (chosen and appointed beforehand) in accordance with His purpose, Who works out everything in agreement with the counsel *and* design of His [own] will.

As we come to Jesus, and accept Him as our Savior we are restored to our rightful relationship with God as a son or daughter. (We become God's heritage.) We, also, obtain an inheritance. Part of that inheritance is the promise of a future and a purpose.

But, what is really exciting is that we get to sit in the counsel of God, Christ, and the Holy Spirit. But, how does that work?

Ephesians 2:6
And He raised us up together with Him and made us sit down together [giving us joint seating with Him] in the heavenly sphere [by virtue of our being] in Christ Jesus (the Messiah, the Anointed One).

According to this verse, as we received Christ, we were raised up with Him and placed in Him. We were, also, given a seat in Heavenly places with Him. This seat is not just a Samsonite folding chair, but a seat of power and authority. It would be more like a judge's seat or bench. That power and authority is way too much for us to handle on our own. But, as we sit in counsel with God, Christ, and the Holy Spirit, we are directed how to wield that power and authority properly in the earth. We are literally called to rule with Christ in Heavenly places so we can affect the world. But, just how close are we to God's counsel?

Ephesians 1:20
Which He exerted in Christ when He raised Him from the dead and <u>seated Him at His [own] right hand in the heavenly [places]</u>.

Since we are seated in Christ, apparently we are sitting at the right hand of God, just like Christ. This is not something to take lightly. We have the special honor to be at the right hand of God and walking on the Earth at the same time. That is because God wants us to CHANGE THE ATMOSPHERE here on Earth so that it expresses Him and His glory. He wants us to become manifesters of Him in the Earth.

With this in mind, there is a simple strategy that God wants to communicate to his people; so that they can live in the victory that Jesus has already given them. This simple directive from God applies directly to our prayers and intercessions. These prayers and intercessions are to include our families, churches, cities, regions, nation and/or nations, and more. Basically, the strategy is what we say and what we pray.

Revelation 12:11

And they overcame (conquered) him by means of the blood of the Lamb <u>and by the utterance of their testimony</u>. For they did not love their life and renounce their faith even when faced with death.

Revelation tells us that we overcome by the blood of the Lamb and <u>the words or utterance of our testimony.</u> The entire theme in Revelation is not only what is going to happen, but also how WE who hear, speak, declare, decree, and proclaim will always be the overcomers. We understand a lot about overcoming by the blood of the Lamb, but have we ever taken seriously that we overcome by the words of our mouth (our testimony). Testimony simply means that we speak out the great things that God has done, the great things that God is doing, and the great things that God is going to do. Not what the enemy has done, is doing, or going to do. It does not say that we will overcome by good works, good deeds, or performance. In fact, here is the best strategy that I believe I ever received from God.

**Being with God does not come out of doing.
But doing comes out of being with God.**

Let me say it another way.

Having a relationship with God does not come out of works, but works happen because of our relationship with God.

What we do, say and pray should always come out of our relationship with God.

Right now would be a good time for a science lesson. What I love about science is that it is always proving the validity of God and the word of God.

For years scientists (physicists) have tried to find out from what everything was made. They've gone past the molecule, the atom, the neutrons, the protons, and the electrons. Finally, they discovered that everything was made of sound and held together by frequencies. Isn't it interesting that the Bible tells us in Genesis 1 that **"God said"** over and over and over again. The whole chapter tells us that God literally spoke the universe into existence. This means that God knew something from the beginning about sound and its building qualities. These scientists have also learned that there is good sound

and bad sound. Good sound has creative qualities
and bad sound has destructive qualities.

James 3:8-10
But the human tongue can be tamed by no man. It is a
restless (undisciplined, irreconcilable) evil, full of
deadly poison. <u>With it we bless the Lord and Father,
and with it we curse men who were made in God's
likeness! Out of the same mouth come forth blessing
and cursing. These things, my brethren, ought not to
be so</u>.

Apparently this is something God already knew,
that our words carry power and authority. It is not
something new, but has been around since the
earliest days of mankind. Consider what happened at
the tower of Babel.

Genesis 11:6-9
And the Lord said, Behold, <u>they are one people and
they have all one language</u>; and this is only the
beginning of what they will do, <u>and now nothing they
have imagined they can do will be impossible for
them.</u> Come, let Us go down and there confound (mix

up, confuse) their language, that they may not understand one another's speech. So the Lord scattered them abroad from that place upon the face of the whole earth, and they gave up building the city. Therefore the name of it was called Babel—because there the Lord confounded the language of all the earth; and from that place the Lord scattered them abroad upon the face of the whole earth.

Verse 6 tells us that they all spoke one language, and because of that and their agreements together, nothing was impossible to them. Literally whatever they imagined, they could do. It is hard to believe that carnal man had that much creative power, but he did. So, God came down in His mercy and confounded their languages to keep them from destroying themselves. This was because man cannot wield that kind of power without guidance from God. This is the only way God could save man from himself.

Does this not make you wonder if this kind of ability is still available to man? I believe so. Science has not changed, and sound is still around. I believe that God wants us to use that ability in conjunction with Him to further the Kingdom of Heaven. That is why it is so important for us to be restored to our rightful relationship with God. This also lends substance to the fact that our words have power to bless or curse. This absolutely means that we can change the atmosphere with our words.

Several years ago someone shared a book with me that explored the effects of sound on water. Good words and bad words were spoken into different containers of water and then frozen. The crystals that were produced were extremely different. The crystals produced from the container over which good words had been spoken were beautifully formed. The crystals formed by the water from the container over which bad words were spoken were horribly deformed. It did not matter in which language the words were spoken, whether English, Spanish, Chinese, etc., the results were the same.

My conclusion was this: If we as human beings are made up primarily of water, then words can have a wonderful or adverse effect on us physically. The old adage about sticks and stones may break my bones, but words will never hurt me... is a lie!

Just how important is all this information to you and me? It is extremely important if you want to change the atmosphere over your life, family, city, region, state and nation. To put it bluntly, it is time to clean up our language. I'm not talking about naming it and claiming it or blabbing it and grabbing it. But, literally changing our atmosphere with the greatest weapon God has given His people, which is our words! It is simply sitting in counsel with God, Christ, and the Holy Spirit, declaring, decreeing and proclaiming the things to be said, prayed or done. We as people of God need to grasp the importance of our position with God.

Remember in Ephesians how it tells us we are seated in Heavenly places in Christ Jesus. This is how important this is. We are not the only ones in Heavenly places.

Ephesians 6:12
For we are not wrestling with flesh and blood [contending only with physical opponents], but

against the despotisms, against the powers, against [the master spirits who are] the world rulers of this present darkness, against <u>the spirit forces of wickedness in the heavenly (supernatural) sphere.</u>

As you read this, you need to recognize that we have some company in the Heavenly places. Why are they there? Not to worry!!!!! **They do not have seats**, and therefore have no power or authority. But, they know that we do; and they are there to try and usurp our authority and power. The only way they can do that is to get us to use our seats with our voices for their purposes. So, if the words coming out of your mouth are not from God, Christ, or the Holy Spirit, they could very well be from the enemy. The Apostle Peter experienced this when he tried to keep Christ from going to the cross. Christ spoke up at that point and said "Get behind me Satan." You see, our words, prayers and deeds need to come from counsel with God. They should not come from fear, anger, dread, disappointment, or foolish reasoning. Our words need to line up with God's heart and purpose for our lives as well as the heart and purpose of God for the lives of others. Our griping, complaining, judging, criticizing, and gossiping are all signs that the enemy is using our seat of authority, even when we are doing it in jest. When we gripe and complain with our voices about the works of the enemy, we are actually lending our agreement with what he is doing. I'll say more about that later.

Let me summarize what has just been said.

1. Christ came to Earth to live, die, and shed His blood so we could be restored to the Father as (blood kin) sons and daughters. Out of this comes the ability for us to have an intimate relationship with God.

2. That restoration has given us a seat, with authority, in Heavenly places in Christ from which we are to sit in **counsel** with God, Christ and the Holy Spirit.

3. From that seat of power and authority, we are to decree, declare, proclaim, command, and demand with our voices into the Earth **what we hear out of that counsel.** (This is effective

because the Bible and science both tell us that sound is powerful.)

4. Because our words and voices are so powerful, the enemy wants to usurp that power and authority to accomplish his desires in the Earth by getting us to speak his thoughts and words.

5. The greatest weapon we have is our mouth, and we need to use it for the Glory of God. Along with the Blood of Jesus and the words of our mouth, we will be the overcomers God intended.

Food for Thought

CONSIDER YOUR THOUGHTS BECAUSE THEY BECOME WORDS

CONSIDER YOUR WORDS BECAUSE THEY BECOME ACTIONS

CONSIDER YOUR ACTIONS BECAUSE THEY BECOME HABITS

CONSIDER YOUR HABITS BECAUSE THEY BECOME YOUR CHARACTER

CONSIDER YOUR CHARACTER BECAUSE IT WILL DETERMINE YOUR DESTINY

So, to begin our journey into changing the atmosphere we need to learn how to Hear, Say, and Pray.

2

The Violent Take It By Force

II Corinthians 10:4-6

The weapons of our warfare are not physical [weapons of flesh and blood]. Our weapons are divinely powerful for the destruction of fortresses. _We are_ destroying sophisticated arguments and every exalted _and_ proud thing that sets itself up against the [true] knowledge of God, and _we are_ taking every thought _and_ purpose captive to the obedience of Christ, being ready to punish every act of disobedience, when your own obedience [as a church] is complete.

When we begin to see how the words of our mouth can affect the atmosphere around us, it may cause us to reflect on why the atmosphere around us looks like it does. It is certainly not too late to make some changes. You may be thinking that change is not easy because habits and learned patterns of speaking will be difficult to change. Actually, you are right but wrong, because to change yourself is impossible.

Jeremiah 10:23

O Lord [pleads Jeremiah in the name of the people], I know that [the determination of] the way of a man is not in himself; it is not in man [even in a strong man or in a man at his best] to direct his [own] steps.

God knew that it was not within mankind to change themselves or guide their own footsteps. This is just another reason His son had to die on the cross and shed His blood for us. So He gave us a gift called Grace. It is one of the most important, but most misunderstood gifts God has ever given us. Let me share a short insight into Grace. If we do not understand how Grace works, we could be fighting a stagnant battle. I did not say a loosing battle, but a battle in which we are making no progress. Grace is not God's tolerance of our humanity, but it is something far greater. We have heard for years the definition of grace is God's unmerited favor, (Vine's Bible Dictionary). Looking deeper into the definition, unmerited means just that, it cannot be earned. But favor means more than God likes you. It means He dwells in you with gifts and power. Most of us grew up thinking that grace meant God liked us even though we were not deserving. A much fuller and more accurate a definition would be this.

Grace is the power of God's presence in us (Christ in us) that empowers and enables us to be what we are supposed to be, and do what we are supposed to do, as children of the Most High God to fulfill our destiny.

We need to understand that if we could change ourselves or stop sinning in our power, then Jesus died and shed His blood in vain. It is crucial that we understand that we are empowered by God Himself, in us, to move forward and fulfill our destiny. So yes, the ability to change is possible with Grace. This is all a part of being seated in Heavenly places in Christ Jesus, so that we can be manifestors of God in the Earth.

When we understand we are valuable to God, it also opens us up to understand we are valuable to the Kingdom of God. What does God think about us?

Jeremiah 29:11
For I know the thoughts *and* plans that I have for you, says the Lord, thoughts *and* plans for welfare and peace and not for evil, to give you hope in your final outcome.

This is my wife's favorite verse. If you squeeze her, it automatically pops out. God has a plan for us, and it is a good plan. Let me explain how God wants to operate in our future, so that it will be good and prosperous.

Matthew 11:12
From the days of John the Baptist until now the Kingdom of Heaven suffers violent assault, and violent men seize it by force [as a precious prize].

I read this particular passage for years and never stopped to understand what it was saying. I started by looking up the word violence and violent. The word violence in the Greek was 'biastes'. This word means a forcer. The word violent in the Greek was 'biazo'. This word means to push in. Basically these words mean *to force or push your way into.* So, if the Kingdom of Heaven is suffering violence, which means that darkness is doing all that it can to invade what rightly belongs to us. Well, does this means we need to become violent and push back? If so, how do we become violent and fight this battle?

This is where we as the church may have unknowingly missed the mark. We have been so influenced by the world, we believe that a weapon must be something that kills or destroys our enemy physically or mentally. Perhaps we need to examine what the Bible tells us about our weapons and how they are to be used.

Let me suggest, one of the greatest arsenals we have at our disposal. These certainly are not the only weapons available to us, but they may be, outside of the blood of Jesus, the strongest weaponry available. We may not consider them weapons because they do not fit into our idea of what weapons should be. But, notice how powerful they are.

Galatians 5:22-23
But the fruit of the Spirit [the result of His presence within us] is <u>love</u> [unselfish concern for others], <u>joy,</u> [inner] <u>peace, patience</u> [not the ability to wait, but

how we act while waiting], <u>kindness, goodness, faithfulness, gentleness, self-control. Against such things there is no law.</u>

Notice the very last sentence of this verse. _Against such there is no law_. Against the fruits of the spirit there is no law. In other words, the enemy has no power or recourse against these weapons.

Over the years I have watched Christians fight darkness and evil with tremendous fervor and passion. All too often that fervor and passion has been expressed in anger, hate, judgmentalism, name-calling, criticism, and even violence. None of which are fruits of the spirit. Even within the Christian ranks, we have demonstrated these same negative expressions against one another. As the Apostle James would say, this should not be. Nowhere in the word of God are we instructed to use anger, rage, intimidation, criticism, name-calling, or violence as weapons for the Kingdom of Heaven. But it says "the violent take it by force." How do we take anything violently by force without something like rage, anger, or some of these other expressions? You can put other labels on it, like extreme Christian passion or extreme Christian love, but it is still the same thing the world uses to manipulate and control. Here is where we need to understand something about light and darkness.

In the world of science it is recognized that there is no such thing as dark, because it is nothing more than the absence of light. When we go into a room full of darkness and turn on a light switch, darkness disappears because there is now light. In the Kingdom of Heaven, it is the same way. When we introduce the light by introducing the nature of God, darkness is pushed back or out. What kind of violence is that? It is the right kind of violence. It is called violent love, violent joy, and violent peace, violently using the fruits of the spirit, instead of using weapons of darkness.

Proverbs 15:1
A soft answer turns away wrath, but grievous words stir up anger.

When we use anger against anger, rage against rage, or any other expression of the flesh to fight the enemy, we will gain no ground. It becomes a stalemate. This is where many of the Christians may be today.

Remember in II Corinthians 10:4, it tells us that our weapons are not carnal. **The weapons of our warfare are not physical [weapons of flesh and blood]. Our weapons are divinely powerful for the destruction of fortresses.** That means they are not of the flesh. It also says our weapons will destroy fortresses. These are enemy strongholds in or on our lives. So, how do we use these weapons? It tells us in II Corinthians 10:5. *We are* **destroying sophisticated arguments and every exalted *and* proud thing that sets itself up against the [true] knowledge of God, and <u>*we are* taking every thought *and* purpose captive to the obedience of Christ.</u>** This is one of the greatest verses in the Bible. It lets us know that we are able to discount and destroy every argument that the enemy puts in our path. All arguments that try to discredit God, Christ and the Holy Spirit, and what they are able to do for us and through us are rendered invalid. What we need to do is bring all of our thoughts and purposes into the counsel we have in Heavenly places, and receive instructions on how to respond and refute the enemy's arguments. Then out of our mouths comes the response of God, just like Christ did in the wilderness. Not only will we be given instructions on how to respond, but we will also be given the words that we are to declare, decree, proclaim, command, or demand into the Earth's atmosphere. These words will be the heart and intentions of God, not our words or ideas. We have never really been called to be defensive, but totally offensive. We are to speak out the heart and intentions of God into the Earth and then watch the atmosphere change. It is time for us to start focusing on what God wants us to declare, decree, proclaim, demand, and command into the Earth and quit focusing on the enemy.

When we focus on the enemy and what he is doing, we tend not to hear what God is saying. Then, what we say is what the enemy is doing, and we are inadvertently speaking out into the atmosphere what the enemy wants us to proclaim. Without realizing what we are doing, we are lending our agreement to the enemy's plans. We do not want to speak out the enemy's plans, but speak out the plans and intentions of God. We can become so involved in what the enemy is doing in the world, that we forget that God is in control, and that what we hear on some news broadcast is drawing us away from God by dread and fear.

During my quiet time, I once heard in my spirit that God was not a God that was against anything. My question was immediately, "What about Jericho?" What I heard was this, "I was not against Jericho, but Jericho was against me. It was in my way, and nothing can stop me and the direction I am going and taking my people." Maybe I can put it this way. We are not called to defend ourselves against our Jericho, but simply follow God through our Jericho. How did they defeat Jericho? They followed the counsel of God and made a lot of noise (sound).

This brings us to II Corinthians 10:6. **being ready to punish every act of disobedience, when your own obedience [as a church] is complete.**

We see all kinds of evil and disobedience in this world today, but we need to deal with it properly. How do we punish every act of disobedience? By responding in complete obedience. Our obedience will automatically punish disobedience wherever it tries to hide. It is time for us to push back the darkness that is in our lives and in the world by becoming the atmosphere changers that God has called us to be from our seats in Heavenly places. Not by the things we decide, but what we see, hear, and know that the Father wants accomplished. Then we begin to be the oracles of God in the Earth. As we come out of agreement with the enemy by not speaking and acting the way he wants, but by coming into agreement with God's desires, the more we are going to see the atmosphere align with God. Remember to speak out the heart of God over every circumstance or situation in your life. Out of the Heavenly places we change the atmosphere by what we Hear, Say and Pray.

3

Blessings Bring Change
Change Does Not Bring Blessings

Most all of us have been raised in traditions that taught us to believe that the way to get God's blessings is by our works and performance. I concur that obedience to God certainly has its rewards, but rewards are not necessarily blessings. Obedience should come out of our being with God, and simply knowing that God knows what is best for us. Remember the phrase God gave me, which said, "Doing comes out of being with God, but being with God does not come out of doing." It is not by our works and performance that God receives us into His presence or rewards us, but He does reward our obedience. Blessings are something completely different.

The title of this chapter was a phrase God gave me one day when I was trying to mind my own business. You know, doing it my way! When I heard that phrase, it caused excitement in my spirit. When I hear things like this and I know it is God, I get excited. After enjoying the excitement and sharing with my wife, I suddenly realized that this statement was destroying a huge portion of my theology and doctrine. Surely you cannot receive blessings unless you change and do everything right. That would just not be religiously right. In times past I have found that my religiosity has not been in line with the heart of God on many occasions. So I began to pray and seek God for clarification. That is when I began to see a pattern in the Word of God. More times than not, God sent a blessing to initiate a change, or enable a change even when obedience was not necessarily in the picture. There is a scripture in the New Testament that verifies this pattern.

Acts 3:26
It was to you first that God sent His Servant *and* Son *Jesus*, when He raised Him up [provided and gave Him for us], <u>to bless you in turning every one of you from your wicked *and* evil ways</u>.

Most all of us are aware of what God did with His son, Jesus, as He sent Him to die on the cross for our restoration to Him. What we need to see here is that God sent His son, Jesus, to die for us as a blessing. He died so we could be blessed with an empowerment to overcome sin. What did we do to deserve such a gift? Absolutely nothing! Let me say this one more time. On top of Him dying to restore us to God, He also blessed us with the ability to turn away from our wickedness and sin, and we did nothing to warrant that. In other words, **"THE BLESSING CAME TO GIVE US THE ABILITY TO CHANGE!!"** There was and is no evidence of change on the part of man that demanded or warranted such a blessing.

What is a blessing? What is it all about? A blessing actually is expressed in a combination of two events. Part of that combination is a gift or deed we do that comes from the heart of God and gives someone who does not deserve it the ability to make a change in their life. But first, blessings are always spoken out before they come into being as a gift or deed. What God did for us with Jesus was spoken out years before it happened. So the purest expression and the beginning of a blessing is the speaking out of our mouths the very heart and intention of God into the Earth. This is where the blessing and privilege of sitting in Heavenly places in Christ Jesus plays such a vital role in our life and in the lives of those around us. Remember, the privilege of being seated in Heavenly places in Christ Jesus is a blessing we did not earn. But, knowing we are there, we must realize we are a people of power and authority. We are literally called to speak out blessings in this world. It is a calling to speak out God's blessings on a world that does not deserve them, but most definitely needs them.

1 Peter 3:8-12
Finally, all [of you] should be of one *and* the same mind (united in spirit), sympathizing [with one another], loving [each other] as brethren [of one household], compassionate *and* courteous (tenderhearted and humble).
Never return evil for evil or insult for insult (scolding, tongue-lashing, berating), but on the contrary blessing [praying for their welfare, happiness, and protection, and truly pitying and loving them]. For *know that* to this you have been called, that you may yourselves inherit a blessing

[from God—that you may obtain a blessing as heirs, bringing welfare and happiness and protection].

For let him who wants to enjoy life and see good days [good—whether apparent or not] keep his tongue free from evil and his lips from guile (treachery, deceit).

Let him turn away from wickedness *and* shun it, and let him do right. Let him search for peace (harmony; undisturbedness from fears, agitating passions, and moral conflicts) and seek it eagerly. [Do not merely desire peaceful relations with God, with your fellowmen, and with yourself, but pursue, go after them!]

For the eyes of the Lord are upon the righteous (those who are upright and in right standing with God), and His ears are attentive to their prayer. But the face of the Lord is against those who practice evil [to oppose them, to frustrate, and defeat them].

Let us first look at verse 8. **Finally, all [of you] should be of one *and* the same mind (united in spirit), sympathizing [with one another], loving [each other] as brethren [of one household], compassionate *and* courteous (tenderhearted and humble).** This is the heart of God expressed about our relationships with one another. We should not assume that we overlook or compromise with sin, but be willing to help all who are in need to be set free from fortresses or strongholds as we stated earlier. This is where we begin to bless people with the ability to change and overcome.

Let us move on to verse 9. **Never return evil for evil or insult for insult (scolding, tongue-lashing, berating), but on the contrary blessing [praying for their welfare, happiness, and protection, and truly pitying and loving them]. For *know that* to this you have been called, that you may yourselves inherit a blessing [from God—that you may obtain a blessing as heirs, bringing welfare and happiness and protection].** Now we find that the calling as Christians is to be givers and speakers of blessings. As you see, one of the main reasons for blessing is that you will reap what you sow. As you sow words of blessings into the atmosphere, you are setting yourself up for a harvest of the same blessings you are giving out. Wow, what would the body of Christ look like if we began to operate like this instead of always looking at the places where people are missing it or failing? This literally means speaking strength into their weakness, prosperity into their lack, healing into their sickness, and peace into their turmoil. Not judging, criticizing, demeaning, or speaking any kind of curse. Remember, these seeds also produce a harvest in your life, but not one you really want. We need to sow good seeds of righteousness.

Since a blessing is speaking God's intentions, then speaking a curse is speaking the enemy's intentions. Remember that all words carry power and authority. And since you reap what you sow, I would strongly urge you to speak only blessings.

I was once told that Jewish children were taught to speak out at least a hundred blessings everyday. There's a story behind this tradition. During the reign of Kind David, there was a terrible plague that took the lives of exactly 100 people each day. The rabbis at the time perceived the plague's spiritual cause and instituted the practice of reciting 100 blessings per day. The plague immediately stopped. Even today, teaching our children and us to speak blessings could reap extraordinary life-fulfilling benefits.

Moving on to verse 10. **For let him who wants to enjoy life and see good days [good—whether apparent or not] <u>keep his tongue free from evil and his lips from guile (treachery, deceit)</u>.** Everyone wants to enjoy life and see good days, but could it be possible that in our lives we are not seeing these kinds of days because of our tongue? That is a question that is between you and God. It is never too late to repent of the past and pray for a new future, so that we will not make the same mistakes again. Remember that grace is the power of God's presence that enables us to be what we need to be and do what we need to do as sons and daughters of the Most High God to fulfill our destiny. Call on the God given grace you have to move toward your destiny.

Continuing to verse 11. **Let him turn away from wickedness *and* shun it, and let him do right. Let him search for peace (harmony; undisturbedness from fears, agitating passions, and moral conflicts) and seek it eagerly. [Do not merely desire peaceful relations with God, with your fellowmen, and with yourself, but pursue, go after them!]** This verse continues to urge us to seek a deeper relationship with God and our fellowman so that we can enjoy the fullness of His presence. God does not want anyone left out; His desire is for you to have that same kind of heart that He does.

Last but not least, verse 12. **For the eyes of the Lord are upon the righteous (those who are upright and in right standing with God), and His ears are attentive to their prayer. <u>But the face of the Lord is against those who practice evil [to oppose them, to frustrate, and defeat them]</u>.** This verse brings us to an eye-opening understanding of where we stand with God. If we are righteous, He is attentive to our prayers and words of blessings. But, if our prayers, words, and blessings are not in line with God's heart; they are curses. Speaking sickness, financial destruction, or calamity toward someone is not a blessing. It is a curse! These words actually set us at odds with God, and He will oppose us. No one wants to be in the place where they will be opposed, frustrated, or defeated by God. We all want to be on His side.

God is calling His people to a closer walk with Him. Not just so we can enjoy a greater intimacy with Him, although that is wonderful, but so we can be God's extension into the world. Not everyone who is offered a blessing is going to receive it because people do have a choice. Choose to speak life and blessings anyway. With God's guidance we can create an atmosphere with our words that give people a choice to change. We are called to be speakers of blessings and atmosphere changers. So, God please bless us with ears to hear, eyes to see and a heart to know truth so we can Hear, Say, and Pray.

4

Speaking Out Blessings Is Speaking God's Heart

One of our son's friends attended a meeting where we taught the message, "Blessings Bring Change". This young man ministered to men in a homeless shelter on a regular basis. Not long after he had been in our meeting, he was scheduled to minister. He was praying about the message because it was difficult to get a positive response from the people at the shelter. As he was asking God what to share, he sensed that he was to share the blessings with which he had been blessed. Also, he felt led to read from the blessing sheet we had given him. You are probably wondering, "What is a blessing sheet?"

Blessing sheets are tools to help you decree, declare, proclaim, command and demand the blessings of God into the atmosphere. These are intended to ignite the myriad of blessings that are in your heart, which God wants expressed in the Earth to change the atmosphere. Blessings should be *spoken, positive, and specific* and *reflect* the intentions of the Father's heart over all situations and circumstances. (**I Peter 3:9**)

As our young friend ministered that night, he opened by asking several personal questions. He asked, "How many of you have had a blessing spoken over you in the last few weeks?" Not a single person raised their hand. Then he asked, "How many of you have been spoken to harshly or cursed in the last few weeks?" Every single hand went up in the audience. To that he said, "Well tonight I have come to bless you." At that point he simply began to read from the blessing sheet he had received. Immediately he felt the presence of God flood the entire room. Every single person in the place began to cry. As the blessings were read the people began to give thanks to God. Sovereignly each person had a divine touch from the Father. During this time many rededicated their lives to God. Lives were impacted as these men received a blessing for the first time. This young man wrote us a letter a few days later to confirm that blessings do bring change. And that blessing would be a vital part of his life and ministry for the rest of his life.

At this same shelter, a young woman shared the same message with the women and their children. Because of the constant commotion, it was always difficult to get and keep their attention. She asked similar questions with the same response. She was amazed as she began to read blessings over the women and their children; the room became still and quiet as the peace of God settled throughout the room. Blessings were bringing hope, joy, comfort and peace. Lives were changed that day.

We have received many testimonies over the years, but one of the most unusual reports came as I listened to a sermon on blessing. The speaker shared about a minister and his experience with blessings. This testimony has so impacted my understanding of blessing, that on many occasions I have shared this revelation with intercessors to help them fight a better fight.

In a small town a pornography store opened up, and immediately the pastor gathered his intercessors to begin praying against this invasion. They prayed and prayed for almost two years, but to no avail. In fact, a few more pornography stores opened up in the area. As the pastor sought God about this situation, he felt in his spirit that God was telling him not to pray against these places anymore, but to bless them. This of course went against everything he believed and had been taught. At this point, he asked God why should I bless or even how I could bless such a place of sin. That is when he heard God say, "Don't bless the pornography. Bless the people with eyes to see, ears to hear, and hearts that will seek God and the truth. And bless the buildings to become structures that will be used for godly purposes." What happened? All the pornography stores closed down within a short period of time.

Could it be that God is revealing His prayer strategies in this season? That we were not called to pray against or pray out the works and situations of the enemy, but to declare God's will, God's way, God's heart into existence. As we declare, decree, proclaim, command, or even demand God's heart, plans, and intentions into the Earth, situations change. In other words, when we bring into existence the heart of God through what we say, we are flooding the atmosphere with light, and darkness automatically has to disappear.

When I grew up, I worked at a farm store in my small hometown. I remember being called one night during a heavy rainstorm. Water was so high that it was running into the store through the garage doors of the warehouse part of the building. We were using large brooms to push the water back out the doors, but as fast as we were pushing it out, it was moving over and coming in around the ends of the brooms. We were holding our own, but after an hour or so, we were wearing ourselves out. Then my boss had an idea, a God idea, and grabbed a few feedbags and laid them across the doors like sand bags. The flow of water was immediately stopped. The waters ability to invade the warehouse was stopped because he raised the threshold.

Some of our prayers have been like fighting the flood of water causing frustration and despair. As long as we just push the enemy back or out by coming against him, he just does an end run. Our authority and power can certainly push him back or out, but if something is not put in the void where he has been pushed out, he just circles around and comes back in another way. It's called a stalemate, and the enemy eventually wears us down. This is where I see a lot of prayer warriors today. But if we raise the threshold by praying and declaring something in the place where the enemy is trying to invade and inhabit, then he can no longer occupy that spot. And, there is no place for the enemy to come back. It is time for us as people of God to start using our prophetic abilities to declare into existence the feedbags and throw away our brooms. Now is the time to bring in the light, and the darkness will have no recourse but to disappear. This happens when we conclude that we **were not put here to fight the enemy, but to establish with God, the things of God and His Kingdom**. By establishing the things of God and His Kingdom we are methodically defeating the enemy.

Personally, I knew a young man whom I had become very frustrated in trying to help. Time and time again, I would try to help him find his way to God, but he always rejected it. He would say things like, "Only weak people need a crutch like

Christianity to lean on." No matter what I said to him, he had what he thought was a better answer. He seemed to even relish arguing to no good end.

One day, God brought him to mind, and I tried to ignore it. He reminded me that the god of this world was causing people to be blinded and unable to hear. I agreed whole-heartedly this was "that" young man. I was tired of going down any road with him because it was always a dead end. That is when God asked me if I had prayed or declared over him a blessing to have ears to hear, eyes to see, and a heart to know truth. I sheepishly had to answer no, but it couldn't be that easy. But, I did obey.

Wouldn't you know it? The next time I was with this young man, he asked me to tell him more about this Jesus. Within 30 minutes he had received Jesus as his Lord and Savior. Blessings can and do create environments in which people can be brought to a threshold to make godly decisions. Blessings do not manipulate people or situations, but they do create an atmosphere in which the enemy's influence is diminished to the point people can think clearly. Do not be a hardhead like I was, but go into the entire world and declare the intentions of God.

There was also a young lady who was a strong intercessor that wrote us about her home life. Her family's home life had deteriorated to where there was not a lot of peace in her house. When she heard the message on blessing, she was deeply convicted. She went home and called her family together. She repented to them for letting the enemy use her tongue against those she loved the most. She and her whole family had fallen into the trap of constantly griping and complaining about everything. They had come into the place that they were not even being civil to one another. As she shared with them the principle of blessing bringing change, they all agreed there needed to be a change. They prayed together and asked for the grace to be bearers of the blessings of God. At last report, the whole atmosphere of their house had changed, and joy had re-entered their home.

So what does a blessing look or sound like. A blessing is nothing more than speaking out the intentions of God over anything or anyone. How do I know if it is from God? That's easy. Anything out of your mouth that lines up with the word of God is a blessing. You do not need to be pressured as to whether to say "God bless you", or "I bless you". Either way is fine, as long as it comes from God's heart or His word. Remember, we are seated in Heavenly places in counsel with God, so we can speak His heart out into the world. Don't forget, anything you say that lines up with the heart of God and His word carries power and authority.

With this in mind, let me share with you one of our favorite blessing sheets. As you read these blessings, read them as if they were coming from God Himself because they reflect God's heart and intentions toward you.

Blessings from the Father's Heart
By: Brad and Melba Burk

- I bless you with knowing that you are a masterpiece created by God, and He is delighted with you. Eph. 2:10

- I bless you with courage to come out of hiding so your body, soul and spirit will align with God's purpose.

- I bless you with the ability to release all the shame and regret of the past for it is a new day and destiny is at hand.

- I bless you with grace to forgive, release, and let go of past disappointments and to embrace the Father's love.

- I bless you with realizing you are no longer an orphan but a full blood son or daughter of your Heavenly Father.

- I bless you with knowing that you are one of God's best ideas and the result of His fine craftsmanship.

- I bless you with a new name that will remove all of the false labels and names of the past. Revelations 3:12

- I bless you with knowing the power of the life-giving Spirit that has freed you from the vicious circle of sin and death. Romans 8:2

- I bless you with the understanding that you are sitting in the counsel of the Most High God, your Father. Ephesians 1:11

- I bless you with the ability to see, hear and know what the Father is saying and doing in Heavenly places for you.

- I bless you with confidence to know that you truly are a son or daughter of the Most High God.

- I bless you with knowing that you were not a

mistake, but beautiful and complete like a portrait painted by God.

- I bless you with knowing you are special, created and designed by God your Father to fulfill destiny.

- I bless you with being everything that Father God has designed you to be.

- I bless you with a freedom from the fear of man so that your delight will be in the presence of your Father.

- I bless you with knowing, experiencing and enjoying Father God as "Daddy".

- I bless you with realizing that you are beautiful, dressed in royal apparel designed to express your position and privilege as an heir of the Most High God, your Father.

- I bless you with being able to express the Father heart of God with honor, integrity, joy and peace: Having Fun!

- I bless you with believing that you are the Father's beloved and being able to live and experience your birthright.

- I bless you with the ability to experience God's faithfulness and to feel and relish the love of the Father.

- I bless you with the ability to trust your Heavenly Father in every season of your life.

- I bless you with understanding that God is the ultimate warrior, and He fights for you, his precious child.

- I bless you with the ability to live in the freedom of maximum fulfillment because you are His beloved.

- I bless you with great grace to climb into the Father's lap and experience His rest and be at peace.

• I bless you with trusting your Heavenly Father that meets every need and desire - nothing lacking.

For you are my beloved son or daughter in whom I am well pleased.

5

Changing the Atmosphere With the Prophetic

Over the years I have seen a great deal of good come out of the prophetic ministry, but also much abuse. The prophetic has been used to restore hope, help guide, lead and establish innumerable good things. It has also been used to manipulate and control people and situations.

I want to share with you a biblically based reason for the prophetic. In an earlier chapter, I expounded on what science and the Bible have said concerning sound. Sound is what all things are made of, and that everything is held together by frequencies. Remember, there is good sound and bad sound. Good sound has creative qualities and bad sound has destructive qualities. Understanding that sound has power; it needs to be used for changing the atmosphere in line with God's will, way and purpose. This is the whole foundation of the prophetic; and why the enemy hates it so much and wants it discredited and squelched.

Ephesians 4:11-12
And His gifts were [varied; He Himself appointed and gave men to us] some to be apostles (special messengers), some prophets (inspired preachers and expounders), some evangelists (preachers of the Gospel, traveling missionaries), some pastors (shepherds of His flock) and teachers. His intention was the perfecting *and* the full equipping of the saints (His consecrated people), [that they should do] the work of ministering toward building up Christ's body (the church).

Many of us are familiar with these two verses as the passage about the calling and establishing of the five-fold ministry. It says He called some to be apostles, some prophets, some evangelists, some pastors, and some teachers. This book is not about church government and who is to be in charge, but it is to talk about the function of the prophetic calling. As we see from this scripture, the five-fold ministry is to equip Christians for the work of the ministry. I believe that pastors should equip the people to pastor one another and to take care of one another. I believe that teachers should teach people the word of God and how to share it with others. Evangelists should equip people to evangelize and share the Gospel. Apostles are to equip the saints for a greater intimacy with God and how to express His heart to the world. Prophets are to equip people with intimacy and the understanding that they can hear God for themselves in many ways, and then to express that into the world.

As you can see here, the idea behind the five-fold ministry is similar to the idea behind the Ten Commandments. At least five of the commandments were about our relationship with God, while the others were about our relationship with one another. In the five-fold ministry, three are about our relationship with men and two are about our relationship with God. And, just like the Ten Commandments, where we need all ten, we need all five functions of the five-fold ministry to be fully equipped. This is by no means an in-depth teaching of the five-fold ministry, but a quick overview to help us understand their function.

The main function I want to share is that of the prophetic. Since speaking out a blessing is speaking out God's heart and intentions, it's not a far stretch to say that a blessing is a major form of prophecy. This is because the words of our mouth carry sound which has power. Can you imagine what it would be like if the body of Christ began only to speak out the heart of God on a continual basis? What if we became a people of one mind and one language? Would nothing be impossible to us as it was at Babel? This is certainly food for thought.

The reason the enemy is so scared of the prophetic is because we overcome by the Blood of the Lamb, and the utterance or the testimony of our mouths. Not our works and performance, but what we speak out into the atmosphere. Testifying of what God has done, what He is doing, and what He is going to do.

Revelation 12:11
And they overcame (conquered) him by means of the blood of the Lamb and by the utterance of their testimony. For they did not love their life and renounce their faith even when faced with death.

We have also been called as kings and priests.

Revelation 5:10
And You have made them a kingdom (royal race) and priests to our God, and they shall reign [as kings] over the earth!

To bring change, kings rule by decrees and proclamations that are spoken out of their mouths; while the duties of a priest are to serve and care for the people.

As simple as it may seem, it is necessary that we understand what we need to do. Now is the time to get serious about connecting with God, speaking out His heart and His intentions. By doing this, we can change the atmosphere of our life, home, church, city, state, nation and more. I bless you with the revelation that God can do exceedingly abundantly more than you can ever imagine, ask or think.

Ephesians 3:20
Now to Him Who, by (in consequence of) the [action of His] power that is at work within us, is able to [carry out His purpose and] do superabundantly, far

over *and* above all that we [dare] ask or think [infinitely beyond our highest prayers, desires, thoughts, hopes, or dreams]

We need to understand the importance of prophecy, as the Bible tells us that it is the very essence of Christ.

Revelation 19:10
Then I fell prostrate at his feet to worship (to pay divine honors) to him, but he [restrained me] and said, Refrain! [You must not do that!] I am [only] another servant with you and your brethren who have [accepted and hold] the testimony borne by Jesus. Worship God! <u>For the substance (essence) of the truth revealed by Jesus is the spirit of all prophecy [the vital breath, the inspiration of all inspired preaching and interpretation of the divine will and purpose, including both mine and yours]</u>.

The Apostle John was so awe struck by the angel, that he wanted to bow down and honor him, but the angel restrained him. He said he was no more than a servant like us, and that we were to accept and express the very testimony of Jesus; what He has done, what He is doing, and what He is going to do. We are to always worship God and nothing or no one else. Also, we are to realize that Jesus is the Spirit of all prophecy, and that all true prophecy comes through Him. As we receive and speak out all truth given to us by Jesus through prophecy, and we express it in the Earth by inspiration, inspired preaching, proclaiming, declaring, decreeing, and blessing like a king, we are being the overcomers we have been called to be. Jesus is not the spirit of works and performance; but works and performance come from our intimate relationship with Him. Bring every thought into the captivity of the Lord Jesus Christ; being obedient to declare, decree and proclaim those thoughts from His heart.

If we are really concerned about ourselves, families, churches, cities, states and nation, we need to become serious about our prophetic role as kings and priests to the world in which we live. It is time for us to function as sons and daughters of the Most High God.

II Chronicles 7:14

If My people, who are called by My name, shall humble themselves, pray, seek, crave, *and* require of necessity My face and turn from their wicked ways, then will I hear from heaven, forgive their sin, and heal their land.

This is not the season to seek our ways, means, traditions or agendas. It is a time for us to humble ourselves and return to the Father's house. We need to confess that we have been prodigals that have misused our inheritance for the pleasure of our own flesh and return to the presence of God. Understand that He will welcome us back with open arms and even a renewed inheritance. But this time, let us get our marching instructions from God Himself. From our seats in Heavenly places, we can be a vital part of changing the atmosphere by what we Hear, Say, and Pray.

Psalm 67: 1-3

God be merciful and gracious to us and bless us and cause His face to shine upon us and among us—Selah [pause, and calmly think of that]!

<u>That Your way may be known upon earth,</u> Your saving power (Your deliverances and Your salvation) among all nations.

Let the peoples praise You [turn away from their idols] and give thanks to You, O God; let all the peoples praise and give thanks to You.

Acts 22:14

And he said, The God of our forefathers has destined *and* appointed you to come progressively to know His will [to perceive, to recognize more strongly and clearly, and to become better and more intimately acquainted with His will], and to see the Righteous One (Jesus Christ, the Messiah), <u>and to hear a voice from His [own] mouth *and* a message from His [own] lips;</u>

God has made known His will and His voice, and the message from His own lips is Blessings Bring Change.

Be Blessed

6

Blessing Models

Blessings Bring Change Instructions

The blessing sheets are tools to help you decree, declare, proclaim, command and demand the blessings of God into the atmosphere. These are intended to ignite the myriad of blessings which are in your heart that God wants expressed into the earth to change the atmosphere. Blessings should be **spoken, positive,** and **specific** to reflect the intentions of the Father's heart over all situations and circumstances.

1 Peter 3:8-12

Finally, all [of you] should be of one *and* the same mind (united in spirit), sympathizing [with one another], loving [each other] as brethren [of one household], compassionate *and* courteous (tenderhearted and humble). Never return evil for evil or insult for insult (scolding, tongue-lashing, berating), but on the contrary blessing [praying for their welfare, happiness, and protection, and truly pitying and loving them]. For *know that* to this you have been called, that you may yourselves inherit a blessing [from God—that you may obtain a blessing as heirs, bringing welfare and happiness and protection]. For let him who wants to enjoy life and see good days [good—whether apparent or not] keep his tongue free from evil and his lips from guile (treachery, deceit) Let him turn away from wickedness *and* shun it, and let him do right. Let him search for peace (harmony; undisturbedness from fears, agitating passions, and moral conflicts) and seek it eagerly. [Do not merely desire peaceful relations with God, with your fellowmen, and with yourself, but pursue, go after them!] For the eyes of the Lord are upon the righteous (those who are upright and in right standing with God), and His ears are attentive to their prayer. But the face of the Lord is against those who practice evil [to oppose them, to frustrate, and defeat them].

God Himself has called all of us to be speakers of blessings, so that we can enjoy life and receive an inheritance. An inheritance of blessings from the blessings you have sown.

Ephesians 4:29

Let no foul *or* polluting language, *nor* evil word *nor* unwholesome *or* worthless talk [ever] come out of your mouth, but only such [speech] as is good *and* beneficial to the spiritual progress of others, as is fitting to the need *and* the occasion, that it may be a blessing *and* give grace (God's favor) to those who hear it.

Proverbs 18:21

Death and life are in the power of the tongue, and they who indulge in it shall eat the fruit of it [for death or life].

(Speak Blessings)

The following are excerpts from various blessings sheets written for different occasions. Over every blessing pray that you have eyes to see, ears to hear and a heart to know truth. These blessings are to be tools to cause the unending well of blessings that are in your heart to come forth like a fountain. To flow forth from you into the Earth and Change the Atmosphere by what you Hear, Say, and Pray.

Life Changing Blessings

- I bless you with the ability to receive and give the love of a father.

- I bless you being healed from a broken heart.

- I bless you with a heart filled with peace and overwhelming love.

- I bless you with the fullness and favor from God and men.

- I bless you with the ability to forgive, forget, release and let go.

- I bless you with a greater anointing for the impartation of truth.

- I bless you to become a man after God's own heart.

- I bless you with longings fulfilled.

Character Blessings

- I bless you with the intentions of God for your life to fulfill your destiny.

- I bless you with an obedient heart.

- I bless you with wisdom to rebuild and restore broken relationships.

- I bless you with the mind of Christ so you see things from His perspective.

- I bless you with the ability to love the unlovable.

- I bless you with sensitivity to God's voice.

- I bless you with a freshness of vision and a God-given perspective.

- I bless you with a desperate hunger and thirst for ushering in the glory of God.

Blessings of Hope

- I bless you with the ability to hope once again.

- I bless you with the ability to enjoy daily life.

- I bless you with a hope that will never perish.

- I bless you with hope and courage to face the future.

- I bless you with good health, strength and stamina.

- I bless you with the ability to be saved and restored by hope.

- I bless you with the grace to abide in faith, hope and love.

- I bless you with the hope to see the reality of what you cannot see right now: God's plans and purposes for your life.

Blessings from the Father's Heart

- I bless you with knowing that you are a masterpiece created by God, and He is delighted with you.

- I bless you with a new name that will remove all the false labels and names of the past.

- I bless you with the ability to release all shame and regret of the past.

- I bless you with knowing you are special, created and designed by God your Father to fulfill your destiny.

- I bless you with realizing you are beautiful, dressed in royal apparel designed to express your position and privilege as an heir of the Most High God, your Father.

- I bless you with being able to express the Father heart of God with honor, integrity, joy and peace.

Releasing the Spirit of Fatherhood

- I bless you with the full expression of the heart of the Father in His word, His ways, and His actions.

- I bless you with the ability to nurture with the love of the Father.

- I bless you with the ability to admonish with all gentleness.

- I bless you with the ability to instruct so that you might nourish your family in body, soul and spirit.

- I bless you with the ability to speak the absolute truth with extreme grace.

- I bless you with the ability to operate in the compassion of the Lord Jesus Christ.

- I bless you with the ability to walk in humility so that God may be glorified.

Blessings for Wisdom and Revelation

- I bless you with understanding and revelation of God's will and purpose for your life.

- I bless you with the spirit of wisdom and revelation and that the eyes of your understanding will be enlightened.

- I bless you with an understanding of Heavenly insight and perspective.

- I bless you with the ability to behold the wondrous revelations of God's word.

- I bless you to receive and understand the hidden wisdom of Christ.

- I bless you to know, see and understand the mysteries of the Kingdom of God.

- I bless you with finding treasures and hidden riches in secret places.

School Blessings

- I bless you with Godly wisdom, revelation, insight and quick understanding.

- I bless you with the ability to make godly decisions.

- I bless you with courage to do what is right.

- I bless you divine favor from God and man.

- I bless schools and staffs with positive peer pressure that will change the atmosphere.

- I bless you with words of encouragement, affirmation, compassion and hope.

- I bless all students and faculty to flow in love and respect.

- I bless administrators, counselors, teachers, coaches and students to be godly role models.

Blessings for a Godly Woman

- I bless you with the knowledge of your purpose so that you, others and the world will benefit.

- I bless you with being able to carry out God's work with honor and integrity.

- I bless you with life-giving relationships that will bring joy, peace and happiness.

- I bless you with knowing that God fights for you, and you will fulfill your destiny.

- I bless you with the ability to trust God as you experience His faithfulness.

- I bless you with abundant godly experiences so that you will never doubt Him.

- I bless you with no fear of falling behind as your godly dream unfolds.

Blessings for Our Nation

- I bless America with a brokenness that will cause a return to the Father heart of God.

- I bless America with the intentions of God to fulfill its destiny.

- I bless America with great grace to return to the purpose of the High Calling of God.

- I bless America to return to its Godly heritage.

- I bless America with divine protection, so it will not be victimized and exploited.

- I bless America with unity.

- I bless America with stewardship of its God-given natural resources.

- I bless America with the ability to be a blessing to the nations of the world.

Leadership Blessings

- I bless our leaders with integrity, honor and honesty: no deceit.

- I bless our leaders with the mind of Christ to see things from His perspective.

- I bless our leaders with wisdom, understanding, revelation and insight.

- I bless our leaders with God-given strategies, plans and keys to solve our problems.

- I bless our leaders with justice in dealing fairly with everybody and every circumstance.

- I bless our leaders with a freshness of vision from God.

- I bless our leaders with new and different ways to incorporate righteous principles.

Blessings for Our Supreme Court

- I bless all those with power and authority to be bound to the truth.

- I bless the Supreme Court to deal with every demonic agenda against the kingdom of God.

- I bless the Supreme Court with brokenness in their hearts over the sinfulness of this nation.

- I bless the Supreme Court to express the full intentions of God for this nation.

- I bless the Supreme Court to protect the people against unjust laws.

- I bless the Supreme Court to bring unity to the nation by being in unity with God.

- I bless the Supreme Court with eyes that clearly see the works of the enemy to destroy families and family values.

Blessings of Trust

- I bless you with rejoicing because you have put your trust in God.

- I bless you with confidence in knowing God will deliver you from the hands of the enemy.

- I bless you with knowing you can trust God in every circumstance.

- I bless you with confidence that God will never leave you or forsake you.

- I bless you with the goodness that God has laid up for them that trust Him.

- I bless you to put your trust in God so that you do not fear man and what he can do to you.

- I bless you to lean not on your own understanding but to trust in the Lord with all your heart.

Uncapping Your Wells of Blessings

- I bless you great grace, strength and courage to unstop your wells of destiny.

- I bless you with grace to forget the past, the hurts, the wounds, the offenses, the shame and disappointments.

- I bless you with the grace to embrace the new beginnings of peace and the glory of God.

- I bless you with the ability to lift up your eyes round about you and see your new land.

- I bless you with wells that will not dry up.

- I bless you with a desire to be realigned with the will and purpose of God.

- I bless you with a well of living water to spring up within you and begin to flow again.

Marriage Blessings

- I bless you with the binding love that brought you together to continue to grow and mature with each passing year.

- I bless you with inspiration to be kind in your words, considerate of feelings, and concern for each other's needs.

- I bless you with patience, kindness, cheerfulness and the spirit of placing the wellbeing on one another ahead of self.

- I bless you with tender hearts always ready to ask forgiveness as well as to forgive.

- I bless you with the presence of God that will guide you and give you strength to endure every test and trial.

- I bless you with a long and fruitful life together to carry out your dreams with honor and integrity.

Children Blessings

- I bless you with knowing you are special and the apple of God's eye.

- I bless you with great favor at home, at school, and with everyone you meet.

- I bless you with benefits of obeying your parents.

- I bless you with the ability to stop, listen and obey.

- I bless you with wisdom to speak kind words and do kind things.

- I bless you with showing respect and honor in all you say and do.

- I bless you with knowing what is right and what is wrong.

Prayer:

Father God, right now I come to you in the mighty name of Jesus Christ your Son, and I ask for forgiveness for all the thoughtless and foolish words I have spoken in the past. I declare all those misguided words to be made null and void, and that the enemy cannot use them against me or anyone else over which I may have spoken a curse or wrongful accusation. Fill me now afresh and anew with your grace to speak out the words of life that you want me to decree, declare, proclaim, command, or demand. Anoint me to be the atmosphere changer that you have created me to be. Anoint me to be the speaker of the blessings and intentions that you have for this world, and its people. Cause me to hear Your voice so clearly that my thoughts would be Your thoughts, and that I could become the oracle and manifester of Your words and expression into the world.

Amen

21633576R00057

Made in the USA
Lexington, KY
11 December 2018